Lifelines 3

William Morris

An illustrated life of William Morris

1834-1896

Richard Tames

Shire Publications Ltd

The publishers wish to thank R. C. H. Briggs, Honorary Secretary of the William Morris Society, for his assistance in the publication of this book. The aims of the William Morris Society are to stimulate wider appreciation and deeper understanding of Morris, his friends and their work.

William Morris Society, President Sir Basil Blackwell, Honorary Secretary R. C. H. Briggs, 25 Lawn Crescent, Kew, Surrey.

Printed by C. I. Thomas & Sons (Haverfordwest) Ltd.

CONTENTS

ACKNOWLEDGEMENTS

The author wishes to thank the following for permitting the repro-duction of the illustrations on the pages indicated: Radio Times Hulton Picture Library: cover, 4, 9, 24, 43 (lower); The William Morris Gallery, Walthamstow: 6, 7, 8, 10, 13, 14, 17, 18, 22, 25, 27, 28, 31, 34, 37, 39, 40; Victoria and Albert Museum: 16, 19; A. F. Kersting: 21; The Robert Steele Bequest, Victoria and Albert Museum: 36; St. Bride Printing Library: 43 (upper).

William Morris and Burne-Jones met at Oxford and remained lifelong friends.

THE PRE-RAPHAELITES

A life for art

'I was born at Walthamstow . . . a suburban village on the edge of Epping Forest and once a pleasant enough place, but now terribly cocknified and choked up by the jerry-builder.

'My father was a business man in the city, and well-to-do; and we lived in the ordinary bourgeois style of comfort . . .

'I went to school at Marlborough College, which was then a new and very rough school. As far as my school instruction went, I think I may fairly say I learned next to nothing there, for indeed next to nothing was taught; but the place is in very beautiful country, thickly scattered over with historical monuments, and I set myself eagerly to studying these and everything else that had any history in it, and so perhaps learned a good deal, especially as there was a good library at the school to which I sometimes had access. I should mention that ever since I could remember I was a great devourer of books . . .

'My father died in 1847 a few months before I went to Marlborough; but as he had engaged in a fortunate mining speculation before his death, we were left very well off, rich in fact.'

Having left Marlborough under a cloud, expelled after a school rebellion, Morris went up to Oxford in 1853 as a member of Exeter College. 'I took very ill to the studies of the place,' he recalled, 'but fell to very vigorously on history and especially medieval history . . .' This taste is not surprising. As a small child he had been fascinated by the medieval pageantry of Scott's Waverley novels, at Marlborough he had read and seen enough for him to leave 'a good archaeologist and knowing most of what there was to be known about English Gothic'. Oxford itself was still a medieval city, untouched by the railway, 'a vision of greyroofed houses, a long street and the sound of many bells'. Here he met Burne-Jones, his lifelong friend, and together they resolved to establish 'The Brotherhood', an intellectual society dedicated to 'a crusade and holy war against the age'. Together they discovered the legacy of medieval cul-

Water House at Walthamstow. William Morris's childhood home, it is now a gallery, library and museum devoted to his work; housing furniture, textiles, books, papers and personal mementoes of Morris and his circle.

ture–Froissart's chivalric chronicles of the Hundred Years War; Malory's legend of the *Morte d'Arthur*; the new poetry of Tennyson and Browning; John Ruskin's brilliant *Stones of Venice*, with its seminal chapter 'On the Nature of Gothic'. By day they pored over the illuminated manuscripts in the Bodleian Library, or scoured the countryside for village churches with neglected brasses. By night they sat intent while Morris thunderously chanted the poetry of the past or of its contemporary admirers Tennyson and Browning. In the Long Vacation of 1854 Morris and Burne-Jones undertook an aesthetic pilgrimage to Belgium and northern France, where they gloated over the paintings of Memling and Van Eyck and marvelled at the cathedrals of Amiens, Beauvais and Rouen. Morris recorded

William Morris aged 23. At this time he was living with Burne-Jones in Red Lion Square and had just fallen under the spell of Rossetti.

ecstatically that 'I think these churches of northern France the greatest, the most beautiful, the kindest and most loving of all the buildings the earth has ever borne'. Walking on the quay at Le Havre one night he and Burne-Jones decided to renounce their intention of taking holy orders and to devote their lives to art.

For a while Morris was content to explore a new-found talent.

'I discovered that I could write poetry, much to my own amazement; and about that time being intimate with other young men of enthusiastic ideas, we got up a monthly paper which lasted (to my cost) for a year; it was called the *Oxford and Cambridge Magazine* and was very *young* indeed.'

Comfortably cushioned by a £900 annuity left by his father Morris could view the magazine's failure with philosophic resignation.

Dante Gabriel Rossetti

'When I had gone through my schools at Oxford, I who had been originally intended for the Church!!!! made up my mind to take up art in some form and so articled myself to G. E.

Dante Gabriel Rossetti. His wife committed suicide and in his melancholia he estranged Morris's wife from him. Gay and handsome in youth but prematurely aged by a life of excess, he surrounded himself with a clique of bohemian sycophants and made a number of attempts on his own life.

Ford Madox Brown was a leading member of the Pre-Raphaelite brotherhood. He painted a number of masterly pictures dealing with social themes and the lives of the lower and middle classes. As a designer of furniture and stained glass he was an invaluable member of 'the Firm'.

Street . . . who was then practising in Oxford; I only stayed with him nine months however; when being . . . introduced by Burne-Jones, the painter, who was my great college friend, to Dante Gabriel Rossetti, the leader of the Pre-Raphaelite School, I made up my mind to turn painter . . .'

Rossetti had said to him that, 'if a man has any poetry in him, he should paint, for it has all been said and written, and they have scarcely begun to paint it', and under his spell Morris began to paint and to absorb the ideas of that group of his followers who called themselves the Pre-Raphaelites, from their belief that after Raphael art had declined rather than advanced, losing in purpose and content what it had gained in technique. Holman Hunt, Millais, Ford Madox Brown and now William Morris drank in Rossetti's theories and even aped his tastes and manners. All beautiful women were 'stunners' and wombats were more beautiful than beautiful women. (Rossetti not only painted wombats in his frescoes, he even kept them as pets.)

Burne-Jones had been overwhelmed by the magnetism of the man who could, in his eyes, 'lead armies or destroy empires if he liked'. Morris himself wrote of Rossetti, who was but five or six years his senior, as 'a very great man'. Rossetti, for his part, regarded them as 'men of real genius'. Burne-Jones's designs he described as 'models of finish and imaginative detail, unequalled by anything, unless, perhaps, Albert Dürer's finest works' and 'Morris, though without practice as yet, has no less power, I fancy. He has written some really wonderful poetry too.'

At Oxford the struggle between Neo-Classical and Revived Gothic had at last been resolved in favour of the latter and Benjamin Woodward was commissioned to build a debating hall for the Union Society in that style. Inside the hall he planned a gallery, above which was a broad belt of wall, divided into bays and pierced by twenty windows. Rossetti, as Woodward's friend, was accordingly honoured with the task of covering this space with fresco and, accompanied by his protegés, arrived to

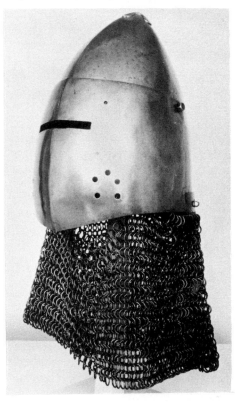

The steel basinet designed by William Morris for the abortive frescoes at Oxford, a single object which reveals his obsessive concern with detail and his love of all things medieval.

work on his chosen theme of ten scenes from the *Morte d'Arthur*. They worked with enthusiasm and a fanatical concern for detail. The following anecdote, from Burne-Jones, gives some idea of the lengths they were prepared to go to for accuracy and the fun they had at work:

'For the purposes of our drawing we often needed armour, and of a date and design so remote that no example existed for our use. Thereupon Morris . . . got to work to make designs for an ancient kind of helmet called a basinet . . . One afternoon when I was working high up at my picture, I heard a strange bellowing in the building . . . The basinet was tried on, but the visor, for some reason, would not lift, and I saw Morris embedded in iron, dancing with rage, and roaring inside . . .'

Bouts of rage appear to have been a regular feature of Morris's character, but it was almost always directed at objects, seldom at persons, and he was always quietly repentant and a little ashamed after an outburst. This did not prevent his friends from making him the butt of their practical jokes, however, and he was reduced to near apoplexy on more than one occasion by purposely illegible letters and mysterious parcels with many layers of wrapping and no contents.

On one occasion he was sent off to sketch a local beauty and soundly rebuffed by her irate mother. Returning disconsolate he was greeted by his comrades with the jingle:

Poor Topsy has gone to make a sketch of Miss Lipscombe
But he can't draw the head and don't know where the
hips come.

'Topsy' was an appropriate nickname. Since graduating from Oxford Morris had neither shaved nor cut his hair. His red mane and bushy beard marked him out as a defiant bohemian. A friend noted in his diary about this time that 'Morris went to Jones's on Sunday night and his hair was so long and he looked so wild that the servant who opened the door would not let him in, thinking he was a burglar'.

The Pre-Raphaelites' deliberately unconventional behaviour was intended to signify outwardly their inner, spiritual rejection of the order and regularity of bourgeois life in an industrial society. Burne-Jones, in rather precious tones, declared that, 'the more materialistic Science becomes, the more angels I shall paint'. Millais's *Christ in the House of his Parents*, now regarded as eminently suitable for chapel or classroom, was castigated by *The Times* in almost hysterical terms—'to attempt to associate the Holy Family with the meanest details of a carpenter's shop, with no conceivable omission of misery, of dirt and even disease, all finished with the same loathsome neatness, is disgusting'. This exaggerated rejection of contemporary society ultimately led the Pre-Raphaelites into narcissism and futility. As an article in their own journal, *The Germ,* tried to point out, they missed 'the poetry of the things about us . . . our railways, factories, mines, roaring cities, steam vessels and the endless novelties and wonders produced every day which if they were found only in the *Thousand and One Nights* or in any poem classical or romantic, would be gloried over without end.' This failure, however, was not to become apparent for another twenty years, by which time Morris had firmly established himself as his own man. In the meantime there were the Oxford frescoes, all-night parties and the cavortings of the youthful, frequently drunken Swinburne to enjoy.

Unfortunately for Rossetti and his assistants a major technical blunder condemned their masterpiece to swift oblivion. Ignorant of the difficulties of tempera painting they had painted straight on to a coat of whitewash, applied while the plaster was still damp. Within a year the vivid frescoes had faded badly, within another they had all but disappeared. Morris was able, however, to draw some satisfaction from the publication of his first volume of original verse *The Defence of Guinevere* (1858). It was vigorous and romantic and represented not only the colour and pageantry of medieval life, but also its brutality. Consider, for instance, the following excerpt from 'The Haystack in the Floods', which describes the fate of the lovers Jehane and Robert, overtaken in flight by the tyrant Godmar:

> *With a start*
> *Up Godmar rose, thrust them apart;*
> *From Robert's throat he loosed the bands*
> *Of silk and mail; with empty hands*
> *Held out, she stood and gazed, and saw*
> *The long bright blade without a flaw*
> *Glide out from Godmar's sheath, his hand*
> *In Robert's hair; she saw him send*
> *The thin steel down; the blow told well,*
> *Right backward the knight Robert fell,*
> *And moan'd as dogs do, being half dead,*
> *Unwitting, as I deem; so then*
> *Godmar turn'd grinning to his men,*

Who ran, some five or six, and beat
His head to pieces at their feet . . .
Critics dismissed the poems as 'unmanly, effeminate, mystical, affected and obscure'. Morris scarcely cared, for he had fallen in love.

Red House

In the autumn of 1857 Rossetti discovered a new model. Morris met her and worshipped her as La Belle Iseult incarnate. She was Jane Burden, seventeen-year-old daughter of a livery-stable keeper, the ideal of Pre-Raphaelite theories of feminine perfection and destined to become Morris's wife and Rossetti's

'Iseult on the Ship'. William Morris's sketch of Jane Burden as the heroine of medieval legend. By idealising her in his heart Morris tried to wish away his wife's working class origins and the moodiness he regarded as proof of her 'sensitive' character. I cannot paint you but I love you', he once scrawled across a canvas as she sat for him.

Red House in Bexleyheath. It was designed in 1859–60 by Philip Webb for the newly married William Morris and his wife. Its exposed red-brick and frank functionalism were considered striking, daring and even weird by contemporaries. Art historians consider it 30 years ahead of its time.

mistress. Henry James described her as 'an apparition of fearful and wonderful intensity . . . Imagine a tall lean woman in a long dress of some dead purple stuff . . . with a mass of crisp black hair heaped into great wavy projections on each side of her temples, a thin pale face, a pair of strange, sad, deep, dark . . . eyes, with great thick black oblique brows joined in the middle and tucking themselves away under her hair . . . a long neck without any collar, in lieu thereof some dozen strings of outlandish beads . . .'

His description of Morris highlights the contrast between the betrothed couple–'He impressed me very agreeably. He is short, burly, corpulent, very careless and unfinished in his dress . . . He has a very loud voice and a nervous restless manner and a perfectly unaffected and businesslike address. His talk indeed is wonderfully to the point and remarkable for clear good sense . . . He is an extraordinary example, in short, of a delicate sensitive genius and taste, saved by a perfectly healthy body and temper'.

The Firm

In April 1859 William Morris, then twenty-five, and Jane Burden, not yet twenty, were married. The couple set up home at Red House, in Bexleyheath, designed for them by Philip Webb (who had worked under Street). Red House deliberately set out to avoid the characteristic products of the day—'pedantic imitations of classical architecture', 'ridiculous travesties of Gothic buildings' and 'the utilitarian box with a slate lid'. Superficially medieval in appearance, with its steep tiled roof and Gothic porches, Red House was no mere imitation of a fifteenth century Flemish burgher's house but a milestone in the history of Western domestic architecture—essentially the first house of the modern age, its plain brick construction undisguised by stucco or any non-functional ornamentation. Visitors were struck by 'the deep red colour; the great sloping tiled roofs; the small paned windows; the low wide porch and massive door; the surrounding garden, divided into many squares, hedged by sweetbriar or wild rose'. It was all 'vividly picturesque and uniquely original' and Tennyson, enchanted, christened it a 'Palace of Art'.

The interior layout was simple, but rich. Open roofs, bare floors and plain distempered walls were set off by bright stained glass, gorgeous embroidered hangings and painted furniture. Morris, Burne-Jones and Webb had designed nearly everything themselves—fittings, chairs, even glassware and cutlery.

Inclination and necessity combined to press Morris from design for himself to design for others. 'The idea came to him', wrote Burne-Jones, 'of beginning a manufactory of all things necessary for decoration of a house. Webb had already designed some beautiful glass, metal candlesticks and tables for Red House and I had already designed several windows for churches, so the idea grew of putting our experiences together for the service of the public.' In 1861 the firm of Morris, Marshall, Faulkner & Co., Fine Art Workmen in Painting, Carving, Furniture and the Metals, was established. Morris, Rossetti, Burne-Jones, Webb, Ford Madox Brown, P. P. Marshall and Arthur Hughes all put their talents at the disposal of 'The Firm', while C. J. Faulkner, a mathematics don at Oxford, kept the books. As with the *Oxford and Cambridge Magazine* it was Morris who put up most of the money and did most of the work, but whereas the magazine died unmourned, the Firm grew and prospered and its success, according to Professor N. Pevsner, 'marks the beginning of a new era in Western art'.

Above: A cabinet painted by William Morris and shown at the International Exhibition of 1862. It can still be seen at the Victoria and Albert Museum.

Opposite: 'Trellis' one of the first group of wallpapers issued by 'the Firm'.

Its first product was a cabinet designed by Webb and painted by Morris which can still be seen in the Victoria and Albert Museum. Morris himself frequently haunted museums in his search for ideas for 'real' things, as opposed to the corrupt trash on display at the Great Exhibition of 1851. From the rose trellises at Red House he drew his inspiration for one of his first and most famous wallpapers—the Trellis; another, the Daisy, was drawn from a Froissart manuscript in the British Museum.

At first the Firm was more or less forced into concentrating on church work because of the hostility of 'the trade' to their products. At the International Exhibition of 1862 manufacturers even went so far as to get up a petition against their exhibits on the ground that they were fakes. Gradually, however, it made its influence felt, driving out heavily upholstered, French-polished monstrosities in favour of the simple, black rush-bottomed country chair, substituting light brass curtain rods for the mahogany 'battering-rams' then in favour. Plain

16

white for interior woodwork eventually 'drove graining and marbleing to the public house'.

Gradually the Firm extended its range to cover everything from stained glass windows to wrought iron bedsteads. Morris paid for a detailed investigation of medieval wall-painting techniques in the parish churches of East Anglia and in the field of textiles his experiments with vegetable dyes were a resounding success. The colours they produced were far better than the crude effects of artificial aniline dyes, the latest invention of

Right: a general view of the Green Dining Room at the Victoria and Albert Museum. Decorated by Morris, Marshall, Faulkner and Co. 1866–7. The decor reflects Morris's passion for furniture decorated with narrative and allegorical motifs.

Tiles by Morris, designed to be used in a fireplace rather than on the floor. This particular design shows the influence of his work with wallpaper and tapestry.

mid-Victorian science, and, moreover, they even improved with washing. In time the Firm even had its imitators; but, unable to compete with its standards of craftsmanship, they contented themselves with imitating its designs—leaving wood rough and unpolished or casting speckled metalwork with mock hammer marks, to make it look hand-forged.

The Firm was very much Morris's personal creation. Rossetti admitted that 'Morris was elected manager, not because we ever dreamed he would turn out a man of business, but because he

was the only one among us who had both time and money to spare'. In the event he amazed his friends as well as his critics. He had been inspired by Ruskin's vision of a community of artists, dedicated to the restoration of creative labour and he also followed his dictum that 'in each several profession no master should be too proud to do its hardest work'. Thus the textiles expert whom the South Kensington museum regularly consulted was not too proud to immerse his own hands in the dyeing-vat or take a turn in carving at the bench. Even the apprentices he took on were chosen because they were *not* exceptionally gifted, a practical demonstration of his belief that every man had the makings of a craftsman and an artist.

His own output was prodigious. As a friend observed, 'his chief recreation was only another kind of work' and over six hundred of his completed designs have survived, covering wallpaper, chintz, tapestry, carpets, tiles and stained glass. Few contain either humans or animals (which Webb usually supplied when necessary); their chief characteristics are an absolute mastery of pattern and a cavalier use of bright colours. As Morris told one disapproving customer, 'if you want mud you can find it in the street'.

Ladies' dress

'Garments should veil the human form and neither caricature it, nor obliterate its lines: the body should be draped and neither sewn up in a sack, nor stuck in the middle of a box; drapery, properly managed, is not a dead thing, but a living one, expressive of the endless beauty of motion; and if this be lost, half the pleasure of the eyes in common life is lost. You must specially bear this in mind because the fashionable milliner has chiefly one end in view, how to hide and degrade the human body in the most expensive manner. She or he would see no beauty in the Venus de Milo; she or he looks upon you as scaffolds on which to hang a bundle of cheap rags, which can be sold dear under the name of a dress. Now, ladies, if you do not resist this to the bitter end, costume is ruined again, and all we males are rendered inexpressibly unhappy. So I beg you fervently, do not allow yourselves to be upholstered like armchairs, but drape yourselves like women.'

The fireplace in the drawing room at Wightwick Manor, Staffordshire, is an example of the decorative style that Morris approved of with its Italian Renaissance lintel and the green de Morgan tiles in the surround.

'The Musicians'. A design by Burne-Jones to illustrate Morris's epic poem 'The Earthly Paradise'.

THE EARTHLY PARADISE

When the hectic work of the Firm threatened to overwhelm him Morris took refuge in writing poetry. Significantly Morris rejected the notion of inspiration in poetry and insisted it was just a matter of craftsmanship, like any of the applied arts. His critics have, perhaps with some justice, turned his words against him and condemned his poetry as being too much like his wall-paper, the product for which he is best remembered—endlessly repetitive. Not perhaps an unfair criticism to level at a man who could turn out seven hundred lines a night after a full day's labour. But it was poetry that first brought Morris fame and to the end of his life any newspaper which wished to establish his identity in the mind of the reader referred to him as the author of *The Earthly Paradise*. This, his first major work, was a rich, perhaps over-elaborate, tapestry of words and images. It was the poetry of despair, a rejection of the contemporary world in favour of the world of medieval myth and romance, the whole work being shot through with archaisms like 'gan' and 'there-withal'. To Morris's intense surprise, and, it must be confessed, to his delight, *The Earthly Paradise* was given a handsome reception by the very middle class whose values he despised and which the poem was intended to reject and vilify. Indeed one critic went so far as to remark that 'Mr. Morris's popularity has . . . something remarkable about it. He is, we have noticed, appreciated by those who as a rule do not care to read any poetry. To our personal knowledge, political economists and scientific men to whom Shelley is a mystery and Tennyson a vexation of spirit, read *The Earthly Paradise* with admiration.'

Whatever the literary merits of the work it provides us with an intimate, though indirect, reflection of Morris's inner agony at this time, for its underlying theme is a recurrent affirmation of the transience and bitterness of love. Morris, it must be remembered had married not a woman, but an ideal of melancholy, languorous beauty. At first their marriage seemed a happy one. A daughter, Jenny, was born to them in 1861, and another, May, the following year, but the couple failed to pro-

Kelmscott Manor, Oxfordshire. Compare this view with the frontispiece of Morris's edition of 'News from Nowhere' (page 39).

gress from the illusion of romantic love to a relationship of real human intimacy and understanding. Jane began to assume the role the Pre-Raphaelites had created for her—moody, silent, unresponsive. Morris continued to worship her as a distant, unattainable figure, a 'blessed damosel'. Others, less kind and perhaps more perceptive, saw her as a vapid, empty, self-pitying hypochondriac.

Poetry was one of Morris's consolations, the other was the friendship of Mrs. Burne-Jones, 'Georgie', to whom he wrote voluminously. His letters to her offer a revealing contrast when set beside those he sent to 'Janey', which are entirely domestic and carefully avoid any subjects which might demand intellectual or imaginative effort. She, for her part, was drifting towards Rossetti, though he was now 'too stout for elegance', and degenerating under the joint impact of insomnia and laudanum. Soon he would begin to exhibit the first symptoms of a strong persecution complex, but for the moment they were able to lord it together at bohemian gatherings and receive the worship of his latest acolytes.

Morris accepted this, refusing to interpret the marriage-bond as a narrow property contract in love. In 1871 he took out a joint tenancy with Rossetti on Kelmscott Manor, in south-west Oxfordshire. Here he left Rossetti and Jane together for the summer while he made a pilgrimage to Iceland, the home of the sagas, the epic poems which were to regenerate his artistic spirit.

The sagas

It was Eiríkr Magnússon who first introduced Morris to the sagas and began to teach him the Icelandic language. They began their work with a prose translation of the *Volsunga Saga* and translations of the *Eddas,* Magnússon producing the first draft and Morris polishing and refining it. Their journey to Iceland was the second great turning-point in Morris's development and the journal that he kept of this visit to the scene of the sagas contains some of his finest descriptive writing. The awesome scenery of volcanoes and waterfalls evidently had a great effect

William Morris at 37, aged by the disillusionment of his marriage and the ten year tyranny of 'the Firm' but about to discover Iceland and its epic poetry. The painting is by G. F. Watts (1817–1904).

on him. 'I confess I shuddered at my first sight of a really northern land. (The Faroes seemed to me such a gentle sweet place when we saw them again after Iceland.) The hills are not high, especially on one side, as they slope beachless into the clear but grey water; the grass was grey between greyer ledges of stone that divided the hills in regular steps; it is not savage, but mournfully empty and barren, the grey clouds, dragging over the hill-tops or lying in the hollows, being the only thing that varied the grass, stone and sea.' Rossetti's influence, and with it the whole air of filmy romance which had surrounded his work, began to give way before the grimness of the sagas.

Rossetti and Jane, meanwhile, appeared to be drifting apart, but his attempted suicide in 1872 brought them together again for a while. Thereafter their relationship was one of spasmodic intimacy, though Jane continued to see him right up to the time of his death. Morris continued to take refuge in his Icelandic translations. 'I am ashamed of myself', he wrote, 'for these strange waves of unreasonable passion; it seems so unmanly; yet indeed I have a good deal to bear considering how hopeful my earlier youth was and what overweening ideas I had of the joys of life. In 1873 he revisited Iceland and two years later produced a translation of Virgil's *Aeneid* in a self-conscious medieval style full of sham and archaism. In 1876 came *Sigurd the Volsung,* a compound of the Icelandic *Volsunga Saga* and the German *Nibelungenlied.* Morris regarded this as his crowning achievement as a poet. It was 345 pages long and, to him, profoundly moving—'the scene of the last interview between Sigurd and the despairing and terrible Brynhild touches me more than anything I have ever met with in literature; there is nothing wanting in it, nothing forgotten, nothing repeated, nothing overstrained; all tenderness is shown without the use of tender work or raving; complete beauty without an ornament, and all this in two pages . . .' Morris was enthused by the saga's energy and freshness, its vision of the simple life and the dignity of labour. Even the greatest chiefs were not too proud to work in the fields or slaughter a cow, while a warrior might be as highly praised for his skill in making swords as in using them. These values were later to become incorporated in a larger vision of man and society, but they meant nothing to the general public or the critics who derided the poem's monotonous rhythms and difficult vocabulary. They still found delight, however, in Morris's archaic prose romances and he too found a refuge in them from the ugly truths of his private life. His last long poem

The Burne-Jones and Morris families photographed in 1874. On the right are Morris, his wife Jane and their two daughters, May and Jenny.

The Pilgrims of Hope (1885–6) is set against the background of the Paris Commune, the great proletarian rising savagely repressed in 1871. Its main interest lies, however, not in its socialistic overtones, but in the recurrence of the theme of love betrayed. The hero of the poem shows a generous forbearance to his best friend, who has seduced his wife. But by the time this was written Rossetti had left Kelmscott nearly a decade and Morris himself had long turned from contemplation of his own

27, YOUNG STREET,
KENSINGTON SQUARE. W.

William Morris in characteristic pose, drawn by Burne-Jones who usually designed the major figures in Morris's tapestries. Having made up his mind to tackle weaving, Morris spent 516 hours at the loom in his first four months at it.

personal problems to an active involvement in the social questions of his day.

Art and society

For Morris the great failure of the Firm had been its inability to cater for any but the rich. 'I don't want art for a few', he wrote, 'any more than education for a few or freedom for a few.' His reflections on the nature of the relationship between art and society led him into social action and this, ultimately, led him to socialism, but his first practical involvement in politics was as treasurer of the Eastern Question Association. The Eastern Question, the problem of the decaying Ottoman Empire and the designs of the great European powers upon it, was a major international issue throughout the nineteenth century but at no time was it more prominent than in 1876 when the massacre of Bulgarian Christians by Turkish mercenaries, the Bashi-Bazouks, threw all England into a storm of political agitation. Gladstone emerged from premature retirement to awaken the conscience of the nation. The intellectuals—Carlyle, Browning, Rossetti, and, of course, Morris, enlisted on his side, while the Conservatives did their best (and it was a very good best) to whip up a jingoistic reaction in favour of the Turks and against the Russians. Queen Victoria wished she were a man so that she might 'go and give those Russians such a beating' and eventually Disraeli, with Bismarck's assistance, managed to slide out of the whole shambles at the Congress of Berlin, bringing home, he claimed, 'peace with honour'—and Cyprus. For Morris the campaign was a complete political apprenticeship. He attended demonstrations, rallies and conferences; wrote hymns and chants for the cause; met labour leaders and even spoke in public himself, getting quite carried away and denouncing Dizzy as 'a trickster, a trickster'.

He was soon able to put this experience to work in the service of a cause nearer to his own heart and closer to his own experience. Sir Gilbert Scott's proposed restoration of Tewkesbury Abbey roused him to such a pitch of fury that in 1877 he founded the Society for the Protection of Ancient Buildings, 'Anti-Scrape' for short. Carlyle, Ruskin, Burne-Jones and Philip Webb gave the movement their support and Morris set out the principles upon which they would base their efforts. It was another significant step towards clarifying and refining his own personal philosophy.

Morris's major allegation was that half a century of enthusiastic 'restoration' of old buildings 'have done more for their destruction than all the foregoing centuries of revolution, violence and contempt'. Restoration he described as 'a most strange and most fatal idea, which by its very name implies that it is possible to strip from a building this, that and the other part of its history—of its life, that is—and then to stay the hand at some arbitrary point, and leave it still historical, living, and even as it once was.'

The Society won a notable international victory in blocking the proposal to restore the west front of St. Mark's, Venice. On this occasion the petition of protest had contained the signatures of both Gladstone *and* Disraeli but Morris's tact soon began to give way before his temper. Enraged by a particularly vile example of 'botchery', in this case 'Gothic' sculptures in a church porch, Morris informed a startled clergyman that 'I could carve them better with my teeth' and had to be hustled away by his companion before the police were fetched. 'Anti-Scrape' inspections strengthened his old hatred of philistinism and gave him a new hostility to property rights which were selfishly exercised at the expense of beauty and art.

1877 marked the parting of the ways. Under Rossetti's influence he had, in his youth, thrown over his prospects of success in a conventional career. Paradoxically he had achieved conventional success and as the author of *The Earthly Paradise* was offered the Professorship of Poetry at Oxford. He declined the honour and instead began to undertake a gruelling course of lectures to working men. The general theme of the lectures was art and its relation to society but their outcome was a new critique of civilization itself, as manifested in its art. For Morris the composition of his lectures was a trial of intellectual strength. The man who had once written 'if a chap can't compose an epic poem while he's weaving tapestry he had better shut up' now found himself floundering—'I know what I want to say but the cursed words go to water between my fingers'.

He lashed out at the ornate products of contemporary craftsmanship—'to give people pleasure in the things they must perforce *use*, that is one great office of decoration; to give people pleasure in the things they must perforce *make,* that is the other use of it'. His general conclusion implied that he would, in future, concern himself increasingly with politics—'both my historical studies and my practical conflict with the philistinism

aking and thief·now am the tree-barks thief :

er twist trunk and leaf · chasing the prey · ·

William Morris's 'Woodpecker' tapestry (1885), the only one to be designed entirely by himself.

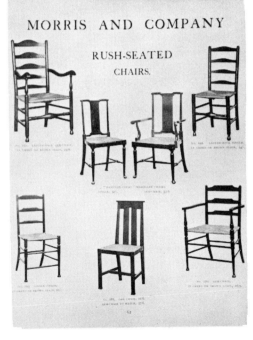

MORRIS AND COMPANY

RUSH-SEATED CHAIRS.

As Mackail, Morris's official biographer points out, the rush seat was not his own invention. In fact Ford Madox Brown probably should be given the credit for the artistic detail of this traditional design.

31

of modern society have forced on me the conviction that art cannot have a real life and growth under the present system of commercialism and profit-mongering'. In 1882 he published his *Hopes and Fears for Art* in which he extended his criticisms of the age—'Is money to be gathered? Cut down the pleasant trees among the houses, pull down ancient and venerable buildings for the money that a few square yards of London dirt will fetch; blacken rivers, hide the sun and poison the air with smoke and worse, and it's nobody's business to see to it and mend it.' His strictures have a very familiar sound for our own ears, with their warnings of environmental deterioration and his exhortation to cultivate the simple life:

'Simplicity of life, even the barest, is not misery, but the very foundation of refinement; a sanded floor and whitewashed walls and the green trees, and flowery meads, and living waters outside; or a grimy palace amid the smoke with a regiment of housemaids always working to smear the dirt together so that it may be unnoticed; which, think you, is the most refined, the most fit for a gentleman of those two dwellings?

'So I say, if you cannot learn to love real art; at least learn to hate sham art and reject it. It is not so much because the wretched thing is so ugly and silly and useless that I ask you to cast it from you; it is much more because these are but the outward symbols of the poison that lies within them; look through them and see all that has gone to their fashioning, and you will see how vain labour, and sorrow, and disgrace have been their companions from the first—and all this for trifles that no man really needs!'

The blessing of labour

At first sight, indeed, it would seem impossible to make men born under the present system of Commerce understand that labour may be a blessing to them; not in the sense in which the phrase is sometimes preached to them by those whose labour is light and easily evaded; not as a necessary task laid by nature on the poor for the benefit of the rich; not as an opiate to dull their sense of right and wrong, to make them sit down quietly under their burdens to the end of time, blessing the squire and his relations . . . But the true doctrine that labour should be a real tangible blessing in itself to the working man, a pleasure even as sleep and strong drink are to him now.'

William Morris—Art and Socialism, 1884

SOCIALISM

This view of the proper relationship between art, production and society led Morris almost inevitably to socialism, which he found via H. M. Hyndman's infant Democratic Federation. Looking back after a decade Morris described his conversion in *How I Became a Socialist* (1894):

'Well, having joined a Socialist body I put some conscience in trying to learn the economic side of Socialism, and even tackled Marx (in French) though I must confess that, whereas I thoroughly enjoyed the historical part of *Capital,* I suffered agonies of confusion of the brain over reading the pure economics of that great work. Anyhow, I read what I could, and will hope that some information stuck to me from my reading; but more, I must think, from continuous conversation with such friends as Bax and Hyndman and the brisk course of propaganda meetings which were going on at the time and in which I took my share . . .

'. . . in my position of a well to do man, not suffering from the disabilities which oppress a working man at every step, I feel that I might never have been drawn into the practical side of the question if an ideal had not forced me to seek towards it. . . . The consciousness of revolution stirring amidst our hateful modern society prevented me, luckier than many others of artistic perceptions, from crystallising into a mere railer against progress, on the one hand, and on the other from wasting time and energy in any of the nervous schemes by which the quasi-artistic of the middle classes hope to make art grow when it has no longer any root, and thus I became a practical Socialist . . .'

One must think hard to imagine what becoming a 'practical socialist' meant for a man of fifty unsupported by family or friends: it meant courting social ridicule and even ostracism, and, more important, the sacrifice of artistic satisfactions to the mundane tasks of meetings, correspondence, propaganda and endless committees. A Marxist historian has hailed Morris as 'the first creative artist of major stature in the history of the world to take his stand consciously and without shadow of

33

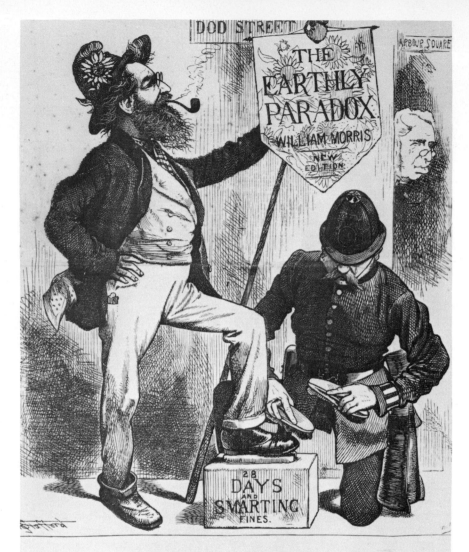

THE ATTITUDE OF THE POLICE.

(DEDICATED TO "THE FORCE," MR. SAUNDERS, AND THE SOCIALISTS.)

A jibe at Morris's intellectual brand of aesthetic socialism. In the 1880s intelligence, beauty and socialism were still regarded as incompatible, but a tearful policeman is shown cleaning the boots of the apostle of the new faith.

34

compromise, with the revolutionary working class'. Whether or not one accepts the terms in which this judgement is expressed, the magnitude and significance of the step Morris took must be conceded. Of his friends only Webb and Faulkner were prepared to follow him—Burne-Jones, Swinburne and Ruskin shrank from committing themselves to the service of a cause which was at once abhorrent to polite society and apparently doomed to early and futile failure.

Socialism in the early 1880s was just emerging from the twenty-year domination of phrenology. This pseudo-science was taken very seriously in mid-Victorian England and throughout the 1860s and 1870s the faltering socialist movement was dominated by its adherents. They believed that it opened up the possibility of objective scientific assessment of personal worth, the first step towards a rationally organised society in which reward would be commensurate with merit rather than with birth. By the 1880s phrenology had had its day and socialism was set to re-emerge in the atmosphere of depression which had settled over the British economy at that time. The potential leaders of the movement were few and, on the whole, drawn from outside the mainstreams of English society—veteran Chartists, continental refugees, middle-class intellectuals and one or two very exceptional working men, like John Burns or Tom Mann.

Morris's accession to this cause was reckoned a triumph by the socialists, but they were not sure what to make of him. The young George Bernard Shaw remembered that 'we knew that he kept a highly select shop in Oxford Street where he sold furniture of a rum aesthetic sort and decorated houses with extraordinary wallpapers . . . And that was about all.' They were soon pleasantly surprised by the attitude of their new recruit. Far from wishing to lord it over the lesser mortals of the group Morris from the start made it clear that he was to be treated just like any other rank-and-file member. Whatever there was to be done, he expected to take his turn at, not as a gesture, or because he liked doing it, but because it had to be done—even selling *Justice* in the streets or walking up and down between sandwich boards advertising a meeting or rally.

In June 1884 he established the Hammersmith branch of the Democratic Federation and in the same year started a series of Sunday meetings in Hyde Park and Regents Park. He walked in his first political procession—'I was loth to go, but did not dis-

The Socialist League, Hammersmith Branch. In the front row May Morris is second from the left and Jenny Morris is fourth from the left. William Morris is the seventh from the right in the middle row.

like it when I did go; in brief, I trudged all the way from Tottenham Court Road up to Highgate Cemetry [*sic*] (with a red-ribbon in my button-hole) at the tail of various banners and a very bad band to do honour to the memory of Karl Marx and the Commune; the thing didn't look as absurd as it sounds . . .'

Morris's lecturing programme continued despite his extra commitments. A letter written to Mrs. Burne-Jones describes a typical engagement.

'On Sunday I went a-preaching Stepney way. My visit intensely depressed me as these Eastwards visits always do; the mere stretch of houses, the vast mass of utter shabbiness and uneventfulness, sits upon one like a nightmare; of course what slums there are one doesn't see. You would perhaps have smiled at my congregation; some 20 people in a little room, as dirty as convenient, and stinking a good deal. It took the fire out of my fine periods, I can tell you; it is a great drawback that I can't *talk* to them roughly and unaffectedly. Also I would like to know what amount of real feeling underlies their bombastic revolutionary talk . . .'

Hyndman's domineering personality and unabashed advocacy of Big Navy jingoism split the Democratic Federation in December 1885. A majority of the Council, including Morris and Eleanor, Marx's daughter, resigned to establish a new Socialist League. Morris became the editor of its journal, the *Commonweal,* and, for lack of any other candidate, *de facto*

'Homage to Morris: Morris and his friends in Elysium' by Walter Crane. It includes portraits of Arnold, Browning, Swinburne and Tennyson. Morris, clutching 'The Earthly Paradise', reclines in the foreground plucking a flower.

leader of the group, a position he neither sought nor wanted. His energy was as prodigious as ever. In the years 1885 and 1886 he co-ordinated the work of all branches, supervised correspondence, attended to the affairs of the Firm, edited *Commonweal,* attended open-air agitations and endless committees and still found time to give 120 lectures and write *The Pilgrims of Hope, A Dream of John Ball* and a translation of the *Odyssey.*

Despite his heroic efforts it soon became the story of the Democratic Federation all over again—grubby assembly rooms, small audiences and blank incomprehension; struggles within the council over tactics; opposition to the gradualist compromises of the Fabians; leaders gradually drifting away, static membership, ill-attended conferences and finally a general drift towards the heresy of anarchism. By 1887 the League was seriously awry but it was to win one last important victory—for free speech.

Many of the early socialist speakers had suffered from police harassment and prosecutions for obstruction. The culmination of the socialists' struggle for the right to speak was 'Bloody Sunday', 13th November 1887, when 200 were injured (of whom three died subsequently) and 300 were arrested. Morris was there, leading a column into Trafalgar Square, the objective of the day's march. The following week Alfred Linnell, a bystander, was ridden down by a police horse during another demonstration on the Square. He died of his injuries and tens of thousands of working people turned out spontaneously to pay tribute at his funeral. Morris gave the graveside oration. It was one of the most moving speeches he ever made but it marked the end of his career as an agitator, though he never lost his fervour for socialism. 'Bloody Sunday' had taught him that small numbers of military and police could easily disperse disorganised masses. This lesson, and the failure of his efforts to make real contact with the masses, convinced him that a great rising of the proletariat was neither imminent nor likely to succeed. The onset of gout, which was the forerunner of the diabetic condition which killed him, prevented him from undertaking strenuous exertion in the cause of socialism. He knew that he had failed as a leader, that he would not see socialism established in his lifetime and so he determined to bequeath to his fellows a vision of the better world which would one day come. The result was a masterpiece.

'News from Nowhere'

News from Nowhere was probably inspired by the best-selling *Looking Backward* published in 1888. Set in the Boston of AD 2000 *Looking Backward* was Edward Bellamy's vision of a future Utopia. Morris's version has an overtly Marxist slant and the tone of a medieval allegory—a sleeper awakes in the London

The frontispiece from Morris's own edition of his socialist fantasy 'News from Nowhere'. It shows his beloved country retreat, Kelmscott Manor, where the characters in the story end up.

of AD 2012 to find himself in a Communist state where industry has been tamed, handicrafts and machinery are in harmony and pollution has been eliminated. Hammond, the visitor's guide, explains the new morality of labour:

'The wares which we make are made because they are needed; men make for their neighbours' use as if they are making for

William Morris at 55, leader of the new brand of socialism.

themselves, not for a vague market of which they know nothing, and over which they have no control . . . Nothing *can* be made except for genuine use; therefore no inferior goods are made. Moreover, as we have now found out what we want, so we make no more than we want; and as we are not driven to make a vast quantity of useless things, we have time and resources enough to consider our pleasure in making them. All work which would be irksome to do by hand is done by immensely improved machinery; and in all work which it is a pleasure to do by hand machinery is done without . . .'

The visitor learns from Hammond that the revolution took

place after a civil war in 1952:

'Bands of young men, like the marauders of the great strike . . . armed themselves and drilled, and began on any opportunity or pretence to skirmish with the people in the streets. The Government neither helped them nor put them down, but stood by, hoping that something might come of it. These Friends of Order, as they were called, had some successes at first, and grew bolder . . . A sort of irregular war was carried on with varied success all over the country; and at last the Government, which had at first pretended to ignore the struggle, or treat it as mere rioting, definitely declared for the Friends of Order.

'It was too late. The end, it was seen clearly, must be either absolute slavery for all but the privileged, or a system of life founded on equality and Communism.' In the event the counter-revolution was overwhelmed and complete Communism established.

In 1955 a massive slum clearance programme began and Westminster Abbey was purged of 'beastly monuments to fools and knaves'. The Houses of Parliament became a 'sort of subsidiary market and storage place for manure'. In time the word 'art' disappeared from the English language simply because it had become an integral feature of everyday life and work. Factories were organized as co-operatives and new sources of power made political and economic decentralization possible. Money was abolished, men lived in true brotherhood and died at the age of ninety. The United States, the new industrial giant of the late nineteenth century, now lagged behind Britain—'For these lands, and, I say, especially the northern parts of America, suffered so terribly from the full force of the last days of civilization, and became such horrible places to live in, that they are now very backward in all that makes life pleasant. Indeed, one may say that for nearly a hundred years the people of the northern parts of America have been engaged in gradually making a dwelling-place out of a stinking heap; and there is still a great deal to do, especially as the country is so big.'

News from Nowhere, of which Morris thought little, is now recognized as his masterpiece but, as one critic has observed, it 'is a picture of life as Morris would have had it, not as he thought it would ever be, and the saddest part about it is the title'.

The Kelmscott Press

Throughout his life Morris exhibited an extraordinary and versatile talent which enabled him to leave his mark in a number of major and minor art-forms—poetry (he declined the laureateship in 1892), painting, prose, architecture, textiles, metalwork, furniture design, interior decor and, last of all, typography. Over the years he had built up a large personal collection of books and conducted careful scientific investigations into the nature and properties of various types of ink and paper. In 1888 and 1889 he personally supervised the printing of two of his works *The House of the Wolfings* (1888) and *The Roots of the Mountains* (1889), and in 1890 established the Kelmscott Press at Hammersmith with the express aim of rejuvenating one of the most debased of the applied arts—printing. As a Renaissance invention, printing as such was abhorrent to him and he strove, therefore, to produce books which resembled illuminated manuscripts. His magnificent edition of Chaucer, for instance, had a Gothic type-face, foliage-encrusted borders, elaborate decorated initial letters and a series of wood-block pictures specially executed by Burne-Jones. Most of his books, however, were smaller and simpler because, although he liked decorated books, he valued above all 'books whose only ornament is the necessary and essential beauty which arises out of the fitness of a piece of craftsmanship for the use for which it is made'. In printing, as in the other arts, he was the pioneer of functionalism. In the nineteenth century it was a revolutionary point of view but it has become the basis of all modern design.

Conclusion

William Morris died in the autumn of 1896. Almost his last words were: 'I want to get mumbo-jumbo out of the world'. The family doctor declared that 'he died a victim to his enthusiasm for spreading the principles of Socialism'. Another said, more simply, 'I consider the case is this: the disease is simply being William Morris and having done more work than most ten men'.

It is not easy to assess his artistic influence because his greatness lies not so much in what he did as what he was. His genius was so various that he never fully expressed himself in any one field. W. B. Yeats met him one day in Holborn. Morris seized the young Irishman by the arm and said simply: 'You write my kind of poetry'. Characteristically he went off at a tangent

The press-room at Kelmscott House showing the Chaucer being printed on Albion Press No. 6551. Morris believed that the artist should regard himself as a craftsman and the craftsman as an artist.

A page from the magnificent Kelmscott edition of Chaucer.

because, as Yeats recorded, 'he caught sight of a new ornamental cast-iron lamp post and got very heated on the subject'. Nevertheless, the meeting was enough to divert Yeats into a fruitful exploration of Chaucer and the Celtic legends. In architecture Morris's mark can be seen in the model estate at Bedford Park designed by Norman Shaw, complete with a Tabard Inn like the one where Chaucer's pilgrims began their journey to Canterbury. A debased version of Red House, with red brick, tile, and low sweeping roof, became the type of 'stockbroker Tudor' which Morris would doubtless have loathed. In book design his influence was felt almost immediately, as Dent became the first commercial publisher to employ a professional illustrator— Aubrey Beardsley. Glass, pottery, textiles, wallpaper and carpet-design all bear his mark, both in Britain and on the Continent. In the words of Professor Pevsner 'we owe it to him that an ordinary man's dwelling house has once more become a worthy object of the architect's thought, and a chair, a wallpaper, or a vase a worthy object of the artist's imagination'.

'Our friend who lies here has had a hard life and met with a hard death, and if society had been differently constituted his life might have been a delightful, a beautiful and a happy one. It is our business to begin to organize for the purpose of seeing that such things shall not happen; to try and make this earth a beautiful and happy place.'

William Morris—Speech over the grave of Alfred Linnell, 1887

BIBLIOGRAPHY

William Morris has been the subject of, quite literally, a hundred books. The standard biography by J. W. Mackail, was first published in 1899 (Longmans); of the many produced since that time the most useful are:

May Morris (William Morris's daughter); *William Morris: Artist, Writer, Socialist*; Basil Blackwell, 2 vols, 1936. Volume I deals with his art and writings. Volume II (with an introduction by G. B. Shaw) deals with his socialism.

E. P. Thompson; *William Morris: Romantic to Revolutionary*; Lawrence and Wishart, 1955. A Marxist historian's viewpoint, concentrating heavily on Morris's work as a socialist.

Philip Henderson; *William Morris: His Life, Work and Friends;* Thames and Hudson, 1967; and
Paul Thompson; *The Life and Work of William Morris;* Heinemann, 1967. The most up-to-date and authoritative biographies.

Other useful works include:
Asa Briggs; *William Morris: Selected Writings and Designs;* Penguin, 1962.

N. Pevsner; *Pioneers of Modern Design from William Morris to Walter Gropius;* Penguin, 1960.

R. Watkinson; *William Morris as Designer;* Studio Vista, 1967.

P. Henderson (ed.); *The Letters of William Morris to his Family and Friends;* Longmans, 1950.

Colin Franklin; *The Private Presses;* Studio Vista, 1969.

THE PRINCIPAL EVENTS OF MORRIS'S LIFE

1834   William Morris born.

— —

1848   Morris goes to Marlborough.
1849
1850
1851   *The Great Exhibition.*
1852
1853   Morris goes up to Oxford.
1854   Morris goes to northern France. *Crimean War begins.*
1855
1856   *Crimean War ends.*
1857   'The Defence of Guinevere'.
1858   Frescoes at the Oxford Union.
1859   Morris marries Jane Burden. *Darwin's 'Origin of Species'.*
1860
1861   'The Firm' established. *Death of the Prince Consort.*
1862
1863
1864
1865   *End of American Civil War.*
1866
1867   'Life and Death of Jason'.   *Second Reform Bill enfranchises urban working men.*
1868
1869   'The Earthly Paradise'.
1870   *Franco-Prussian War.*
1871   Morris visits Iceland. Tenant of Kelmscott Manor. *Paris Commune crushed.*
1872
1873   Revisits Iceland.
1874
1875   Translation of Virgil's 'Aeneid'.   Morris, Marshall, Faulkner & Co. dissolved and continued as Morris & Co.
1876   'Sigurd the Volsung'.
1877   Society for the Protection of Ancient Buildings.
1878   Tenant of Kelmscott House, Upper Mall, Hammersmith.
1879
1880
1881   Merton Abbey Works established.

1882 'Hopes and Fears for Art'.
1883 *Social Democratic Federation established.*
1884 'Art and Socialism'. *Third Reform Bill enfranchises rural poor.*
1885 Edits 'The Commonweal'.
1886
1887 'A Dream of John Ball'. *Trafalgar Square riots.*
1888
1889
1890 Kelmscott Press established.
1891 'News from Nowhere'.
1892
1893
1894 'How I Became a Socialist'.
1895
1896 Death of William Morris.

FINDING OUT ABOUT WILLIAM MORRIS

The Victoria and Albert Museum, where Morris himself often wandered in search of inspiration, contains both furniture and textiles by Morris and his associates.

Kelmscott Manor, Oxfordshire, has a considerable collection of Morris's work, and Red House, his home at Bexleyheath, Kent, is lovingly cared for by its present owners.

Wightwick Manor, three miles west of Wolverhampton, is described by the National Trust as 'a William Morris and Pre-Raphaelite Period Piece'. In addition to furniture, carpets and wallpapers produced by the Firm, there are paintings by Holman Hunt, Millais, Ruskin and Rossetti and books from the Kelmscott Press.

Undoubtedly the finest and most comprehensive collection of Morris's work can be found at Water House, Forest Road, Walthamstow. This fine Georgian building, the family home of the Morrises from 1848 to 1856, contains such treasures as the steel helmet made by Morris, his Woodpecker tapestry, dozens of personal mementoes, his complete works and hundreds of sketches and designs. In addition the William Morris Gallery houses furniture by Mackmurdo, tiles by de Morgan, sketches by Burne-Jones and many other Pre-Raphaelite treasures.

47

INDEX